PIANO LITERATURE Volume Four

for the EARLY ADVANCED GRADES

COMPILED and EDITED by **James Bastien**

Baroque

Classical

Romantic

Contemporary

GWM

GENERAL WORDS & MUSIC CO. — NEIL A. KJOS MUSIC COMPANY, **Publishers**

FOREWORD

- The compositions in this collection provide suitable material for study, recital, auditions and musical recreation at the early advanced level. Constant exposure to the literature of the four great eras of music represented in this volume will enable the student to acquire the necessary feeling for imaginative interpretations of the various musical styles that span nearly three centuries.

- The selections are set in chronological order and all compositions are in their original form. Phrasing, fingering and dynamic markings are often editorial additions—especially to some of the music in the Baroque era. These signs were added for increased clarity of structure and for easier understanding of the mood of the compositions.

- This volume is a sequel to PIANO LITERATURE, Volumes 1-3. The continuous, consistent and systematic grading throughout all of these collections has been of prime importance.

ISBN 0-8497-6054-2

TITLE INDEX
ALPHABETICAL LISTING

COMPOSER INDEX
CHRONOLOGICAL LISTING

Invention No. 13

Johann Sebastian Bach

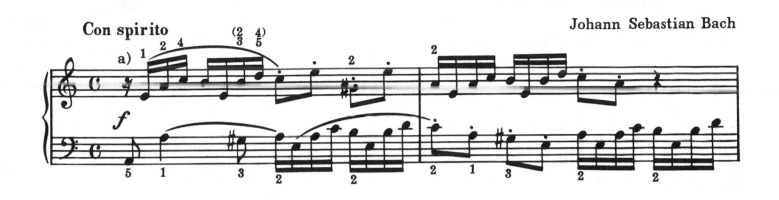

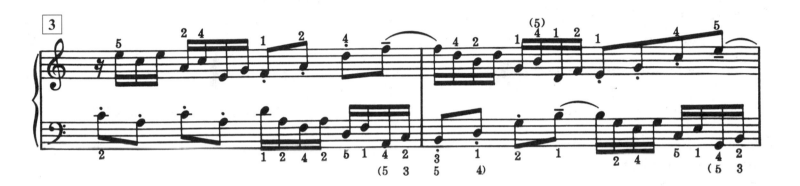

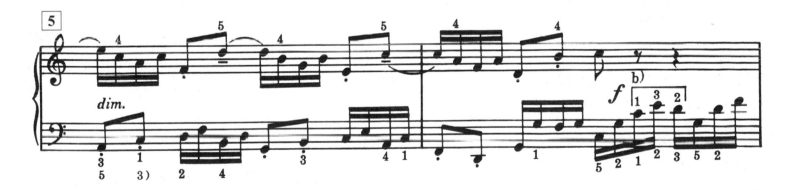

a) Phrasing throughout is similar.
b) The right hand may play these three notes to facilitate this awkward passage (optional).

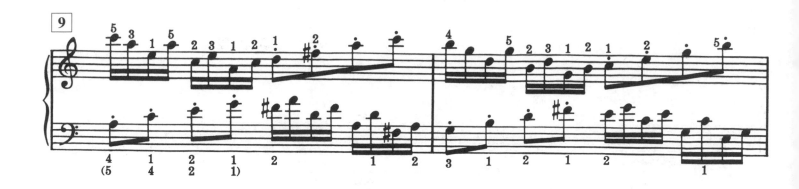

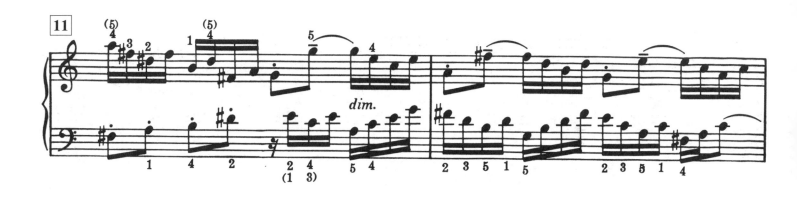

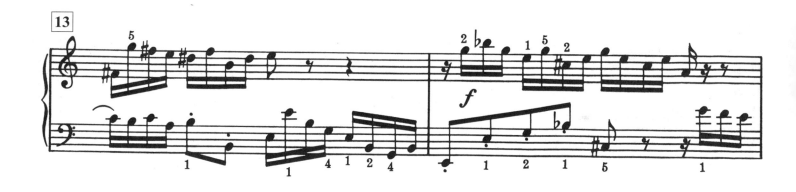

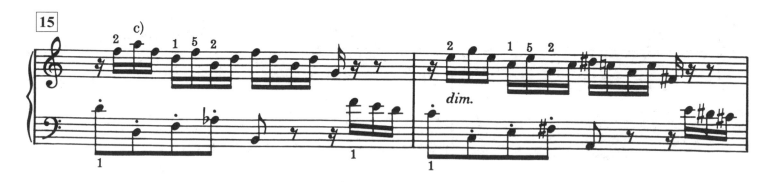

c) Some editions have A♭. The Autograph has A♮.

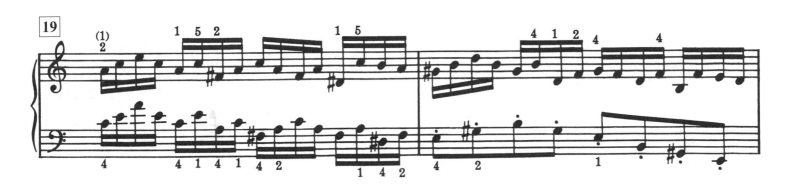

Invention No. 14

Johann Sebastian Bach

a) Terraced dynamics are optional.

Sonatina

Allegretto

George Frideric Handel

Sonata

Allegro maestoso

Domenico Scarlatti
Longo 58

a) Pedal is optional.

con Ped.

a) Suite in A Major

Allemande

Georg Philipp Telemann

Moderato

a) This suite is from a book J. S. Bach began for his eldest son, Wilhelm Friedemann, who was then a little over nine years old. The book is titled *Clavier-Buchlein vor Wilhelm Friedemann Bach (Little Clavier Book for Wilhelm Friedemann Bach)*. The pieces are by J. S. Bach, other composers, and some whose origins are unknown. This suite is attributed to Telemann.

b) Some editions give the realization of this trill (and others similar) as: ♩♩♩♩♩ This is the standard realization of the trill which may be used if it can be played in this manner without difficulty. However, because of the various positions of this figure throughout the "Allemande", the extra note (repetition of the second note) in the trill is difficult, and the version above is suggested. If embellishments pose a problem for the student in the "Allemande", they may be omitted with the exception of the cadence trills.

Courante

Con moto

a) See footnote b on page 16. This trill may be played in the same manner.

b) The roll is optional.

c) The roll is optional.

Gigue

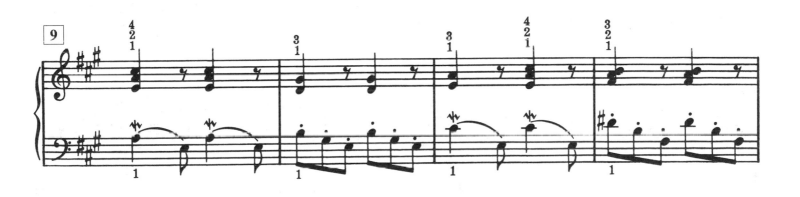

a) The roll is optional.

b) The roll is optional.

Sonata

Ludwig van Beethoven
Op. 49, No. 2

Allegro, ma non troppo

Tempo di Menuetto

Sonata

Domenico Cimarosa

Sonata

Joseph Haydn
Hoboken XVI: 7

Minuet

Moderato

TRIO

Minuet D.C. al Fine

Finale

Vivace

Sonata

Wolfgang Amadeus Mozart
K. 545

Rondo

Allegretto

Rondo Alla Turca

from Sonata in A, K. 331

Wolfgang Amadeus Mozart

a) Polonaise in G Minor

Allegro maestoso

Frédéric Chopin

a) This little polonaise was published in 1817 when Chopin was only seven years old.

Polonaise D C al fine

Prelude in A Major

Frédéric Chopin
Op. 28, No. 7

a) The pedal changes on the second beat are added by the editor. Although Chopin wrote one pedal for each harmony, a quick pedal change on the second beat is advised because of the additional resonance of the modern piano.

b) This chord may be played in the following ways:

Large Hands   Small Hands

Prelude in C Minor

Frédéric Chopin
Op. 28, No. 20

a) Although it was not indicated in Chopin's Autograph, a flat sign appears before the E in some editions. According to the editors of the Oxford edition, Chopin was reported to have written it in a copy belonging to one of his pupils.

Prelude in E Minor

Frédéric Chopin
Op. 28, No. 4

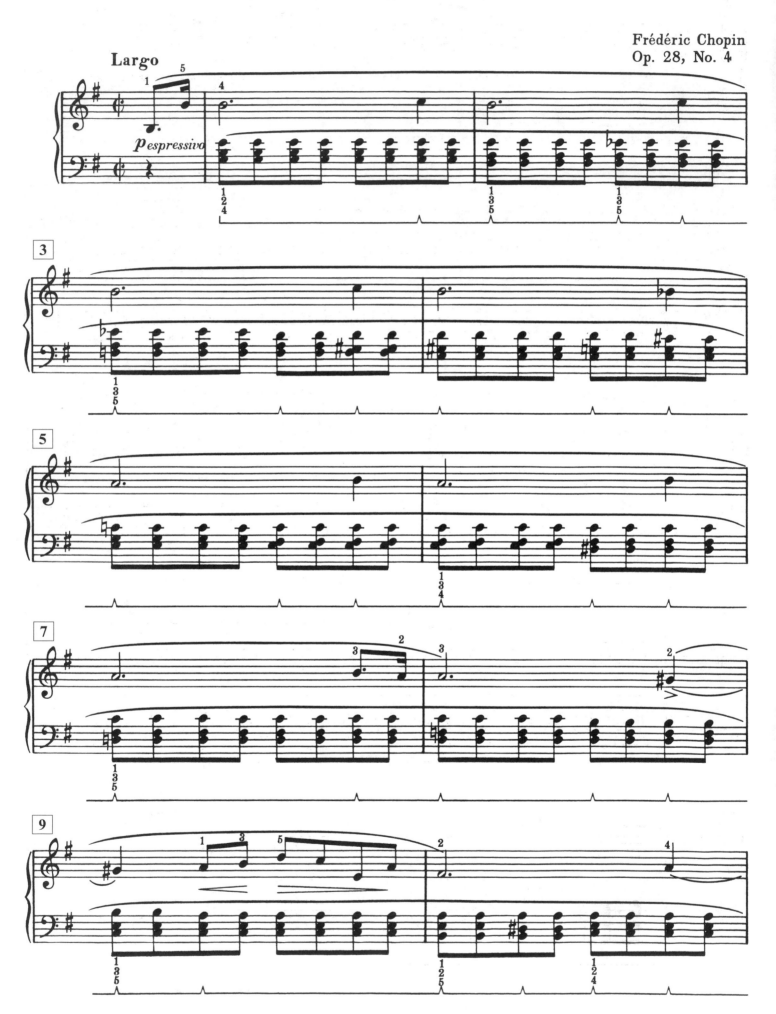

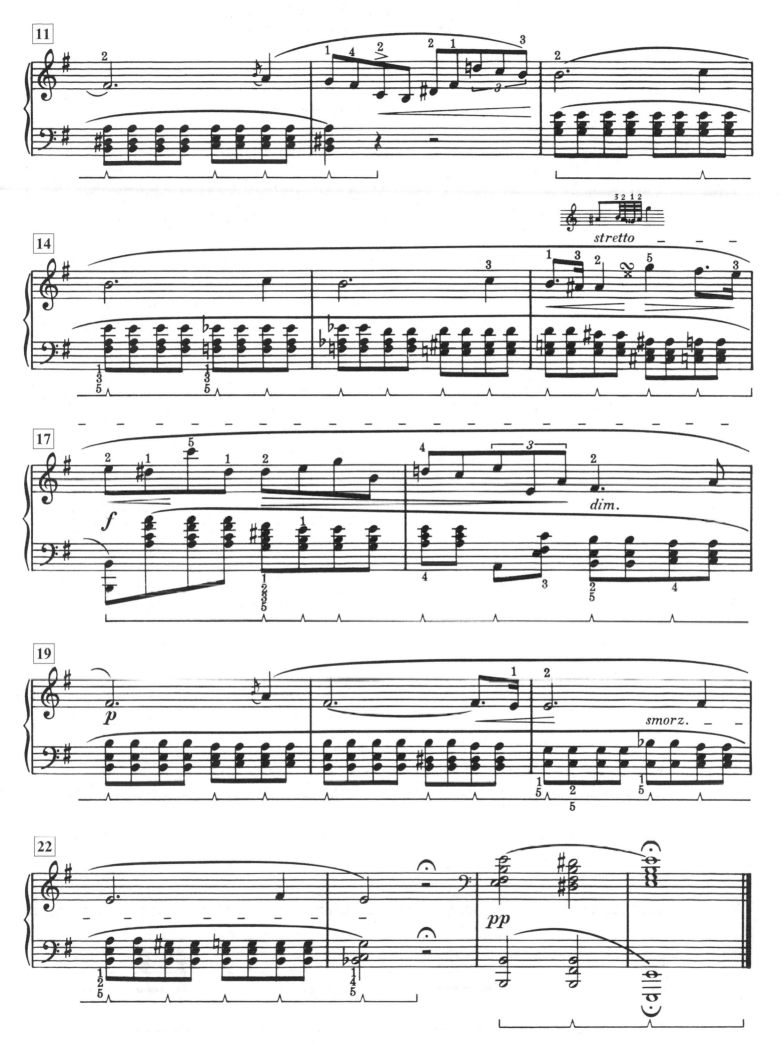

Prelude in B Minor

Frédéric Chopin
Op. 28, No. 6

Tarantella

from "Songs Without Words"

Felix Mendelssohn-Bartholdy
Op. 102, No. 3

Valse Mélancolique

Vladimir Rebikoff
Op. 2, No. 3

Curious Story

Stephen Heller
Op. 138, No. 9

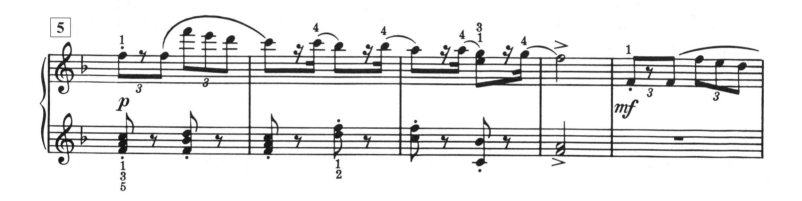

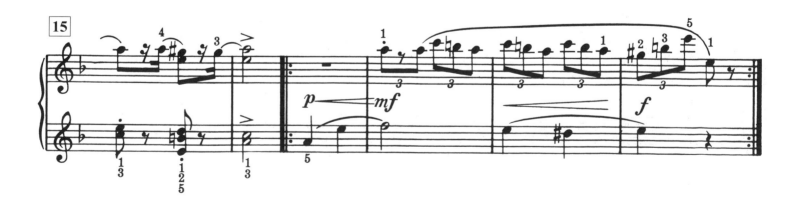

Waltz in C Major

Franz Schubert
Op. 77, No. 1

Waltz in A Minor

Franz Schubert
Op. 77, No. 9

Scherzo in B♭ Major

Franz Schubert
DV 593

TRIO

D. C. al Fine

a) Knight Ruppert

from "Album for the Young"

Robert Schumann
Op. 68, No. 12

a) Knight Ruppert is a translation from the German, *Knecht Ruprecht*, a legendary figure who customarily appears at Christmas time to take children to task for misbehavior — a sort of "anti-Santa."

Blindman's Buff

from "Scenes from Childhood"

Robert Schumann
Op. 15, No. 3

Allegro scherzando

An Important Event

from "Scenes from Childhood"

Robert Schumann
Op. 15, No. 6

Allegro maestoso

con Ped.

Song of the Lark
from "Children's Album"

Peter Ilyich Tchaikovsky
Op. 39, No. 22

Sonatina

Allegro assai e lusingando

Dmitri Kabalevsky
Op. 13, No. 1

Four Rondos
1. March

Dmitri Kabalevsky
Op. 60, No. 1

Allegro marziale

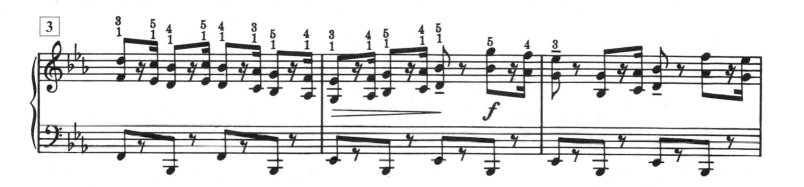

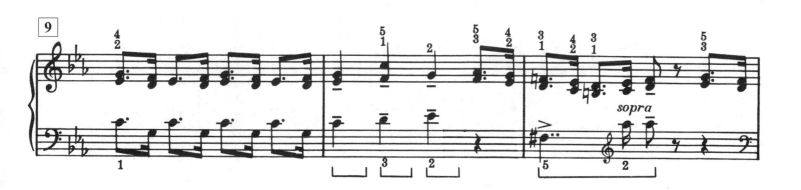

2. Dance

Dmitri Kabalevsky
Op. 60, No. 2

3. Song

Dmitri Kabalevsky
Op. 60, No. 3

4. Toccata

Dmitri Kabalevsky
Op. 60, No. 4

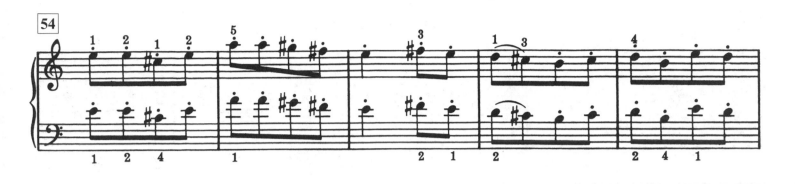

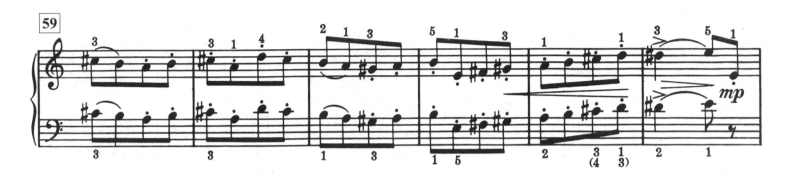

Variations

Introduction
Allegretto brioso

Dmitri Kabalevsky
Op. 40, No. 1

Theme

Variation 1

Variation 11

Waltz
from "Adventures of Ivan"

Aram Khachaturian

Gymnopédie
No. 1

Erik Satie

Lent et douloureux

Prelude

Dmitri Shostakovich
Op. 34, No. 19

Fugue in Classic Style

Nicolas Miaskovsky

Bagatelle

Alexander Tcherepnin
Op. 5, No. 1

Allegro marziale

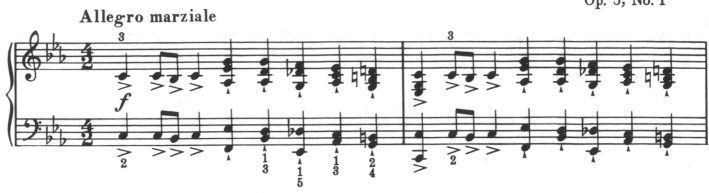